WILLIAM BURGES
1827–81

Matthew Williams

WILLIAM BURGES was one of the most imaginative designers of the 19th century. A plump, bustling, short-sighted little bachelor, Burges was regarded by many as an eccentric. He had a passion for the world of the Middle Ages, and especially for Gothic architecture. Calling himself an 'art-architect', he placed great importance upon the decoration and furnishing of his buildings. Burges's taste for rich effects in sculpture, murals, mosaic and stained glass made him an extremely expensive architect to employ. Consequently, few people could afford him.

'Billy' Burges was born near London in 1827, the son of a marine engineer. His enthusiasm for medieval architecture dated from his youth, and at the age of 17 he was articled to the architect Edward Blore.

Burges had his own highly individual style combined with an explosive temper, so it isn't surprising that his early partnership with another architect was short-lived before he set up in practice by himself in London. He had a keen sense of fun, and his designs are often enlivened with jokes and puns.

His scholarly reputation enabled him to undertake restoration schemes; ecclesiastical and secular projects gradually followed, and by the time he was in his 40s, Burges was working on several major commissions, including a cathedral in Ireland, a country house, churches and his extraordinary Welsh castles. He died in 1881, aged 53, in the house he had built for himself only a short time before.

T: *William Burges wearing dieval costume, painted on library bookcases by the st Fred Weekes. Beside him model of Tower House, his don home.*

LEFT: *The Burges Decanter, now on display in the Fitzwilliam Museum, Cambridge. Antique coins, seals and gemstones are all incorporated into this extraordinary claret jug, which Burges designed for himself.*

1

THE VICTORIAN GOTHIC REVIVAL

The Victorian age was one of immense change in Britain. Industrialization encouraged the growth of cities, and many felt that an appropriate architectural style was needed that would define the new Britain. Until the 1840s, most public buildings, churches and houses continued to be built in the classical style that had dominated for so long. Gothic architecture was essentially both northern European and Christian in origin, and – with its evident use of strong materials such as stone and its opportunities for craftsmanship – it was thought to be highly appropriate as a national style for Britain. Many people, however, still favoured the classical taste, and the debate became known as 'the battle of the styles'.

Burges, of course, was completely committed to Gothic, and bemoaned 'the want of a distinctive style in the 19th century'. There had been a revival of interest in Gothic architecture in the 18th century, but buildings in the 'Gothick' taste tended to be rather more concerned with creating a medieval effect than seriously copying the past. Scholarly studies of Gothic architecture by A.W.N. Pugin and John Ruskin proved influential, and by the 1860 Gothic Revival appeared to emerge the dominant architectural style, and became particularly popular for civil and religious buildings.

BELOW: Queen Victoria and Prince Albert at the Bal Costume, 12 May 1842, by Sir Edwin Landseer (detail). They are dressed as Queen Philippa and King Edward III.

The Gothic style was popularized
architects such as Sir George
bert Scott, Alfred Waterhouse and
. Street – and, of course, William
ges. The ideas of the Ecclesiological
iety also gave impetus to the
thic Revival. A large number
ew churches were built and
orately decorated with stained
s, carvings, murals and metalwork.

ABOVE: *This Gothic memorial to Prince Albert was designed by
Sir George Gilbert Scott and dates from 1862–76; it glitters with
mosaics, carved stonework and gilding. Unfashionable for many
years, it was restored in the late 1990s.*

ABOVE LEFT: *Following a disastrous fire in 1834, the Houses of
Parliament were rebuilt (1837–67) in the Gothic Revival style by
Charles Barry and A.W.N. Pugin.*

Gothic predominated until the late
1870s, when its popularity began to
wane in favour of the 'Queen Anne'
style. By the 1890s, it was claimed
that 'the Gothic Revival has gone the
way of all revivals' and was dead.
However, many of its aspirations –
for example, a respect for the
craftsmanship of the past – were later
adopted by the architects of the Arts
and Crafts movement.

LEFT: *Tyntesfield, near Bristol, was rebuilt
by the architect John Norton for the Gibbs
family in 1863–6. The respectable solidity
of Gothic was appreciated by those
designing country houses.*

3

Early Commissions

B urges visited Normandy and Belgium in 1849, and Germany the following year. He made measured drawings, as well as filling the little notebooks he always carried with sketched details of medieval buildings.

His serious love of French architecture dates from this time, and it must have been a triumphant moment when in 1856 he and Henry Clutton won the architectural competition to build a cathedral at Lille in France. Sadly, their design was never built, a fate shared with Burges's designs for the Crimea Memorial Church in Constantinople. One early commission must have proved congenial, however – the restoration of the 11th-century

ABOVE: *Burges transformed Waltham Abbey from 1859. His sculpture, stained glass and ceiling painted with astrological symbols complement the robust original architecture.*

RIGHT: *Worcester College Chapel, Oxford. Burges disliked most Georgian classical architecture, which he called 'debased'. His reaction was to bring colour and iconography into what had been a plain 18th-century building.*

Waltham Abbey in Essex. In 1859, Burges redesigned the east wall, inserting a rose window filled with stained glass and adding a ceiling decorated with signs of the zodiac.

Waltham was an ancient building, but in 1864 Burges was faced with the difficulty of transforming a Georgian neo-classical structure. This was the chapel of Worcester College, Oxford, designed by James Wyatt in the 1770s. The plain, chaste chapel was completely reordered; wall decorations were painted, stained glass was inserted into the windows and superb mosaics covered the floors. The carved wooden pews are a special delight. A splendid lectern and candelabra in alabaster and bronze were added. Burges also redesigned the College Hall but, sadly, most of his work has been swept away by later alterations. The chapel, however, remains intact.

Burges was keen to perform a similar scheme at St Paul's Cathedral. By the 1870s, Wren's architecture was extremely unfashionable, and Burges planned to transform it with an elaborate and colourful scheme; but there was something of an outcry in the press, and Burges's proposals were quietly dropped.

Domestic commissions were fewer, although Burges had redesigned a house called Gayhurst in Buckinghamshire for Lord and Lady Carrington in 1858. Although only parts of Burges's original scheme have survived, one of his oddest buildings – a privy built for male servants – is still to be seen.

ABOVE: *The privy at Gayhurst is surmounted by a carving of Cerberus, the legendary dog who guarded the gates of hell. Cerberus has eyes of red glass in each of his three heads!*

LEFT: *The carved animals on the Worcester College Chapel pews are a hallmark of Burges's work – animals, birds and insects appear in many of his decorative schemes.*

St Fin Barre's Cathedral

I n 1863, Burges won an architectural competition to build the new cathedral of St Fin Barre in Cork, Ireland. This relatively small but exceedingly powerful-looking building was designed in his beloved French Gothic style. Three great spires of Cork limestone rise above and dominate the city.

BELOW: *St Fin Barre's Cathedral's nave is narrow, but extremely high, giving an impression of grandeur. 'Here is real architectural power,' wrote one reviewer.*

Work of this immense scale and quality was never going to be cheap – Burges himself once wrote that 'there are no bargains in art'. The budget for the building of the cathedral was originally £15,000, which Burges certainly expected to exceed – but its total cost was over £100,000. However, the Dean and Chapter got their money's worth, and the interior is equally impressive.

Perhaps the most striking feature is the glass. Burges excelled at stained glass, and unlike many churches where glass is added randomly at different dates, here Burges presents a single iconographic scheme. His sketches were mostly cartooned by his friend H.W. Lonsdale, who worked on nearly all of Burges's major projects. The glass itself was made by Gualbert Saunders, who had worked in Burges's office before setting up as a stained-glass maker. Saunders' superb sense of vivid colour helps give the glass its great power.

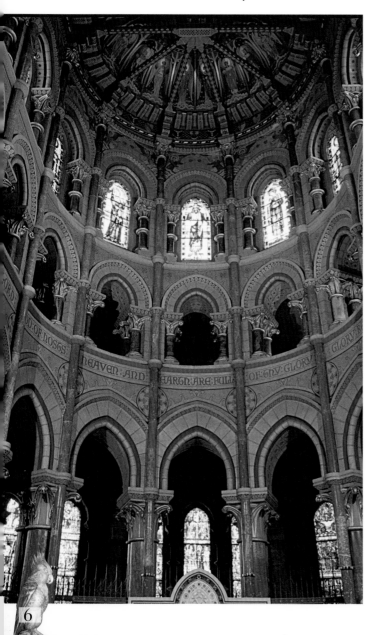

ABOVE: *Daniel's vision of the four beasts (1880). Designs for the cathedral's stained glass were sketched by Burges, then handed to one of his tea of artists to make into cartoons; these in turn wei given to the glass-maker.*

Yorkshire Churches

Burges designed two churches in Yorkshire, both for private estates near Ripon. The churches were built as the result of a tragedy – the murder of Frederick Grantham Vyner in 1870. His mother built the Church of Christ the Consoler at Skelton, and his sister, the Marchioness of Ripon, built St Mary's Studley Royal.

Despite being quite small, St Mary's Studley Royal is an ecclesiastical masterpiece. It was an expensive building, and Burges's splendid interior makes lavish use of marble, superb mosaic floors, frescoes and some of his finest stained glass. It has an elaborate theme of 'paradise lost and paradise regained'. The chancel is the most decorative part of the church, and is dominated by a gilded dome in the ceiling.

The sister Church of Christ the Consoler, Skelton, which is part of the Newby Hall Estate, shares much

LEFT: *The Church of Christ the Consoler, Skelton, is early-English in detail, and the exterior decoration prepares the visitor for the exuberance found in the interior.*

BELOW: *Both St Mary's Studley Royal and Christ the Consoler, Skelton, are built of local stone.*

INSET BELOW: *Although Burges designed other English churches, his finest work is in Yorkshire. The carving is by his favourite sculptor, Thomas Nicholls of Lambeth.*

of the richness of St Mary's. Only very slightly plainer than Studley Royal, it demonstrates Burges's taste for 'muscular' Gothic with its bold details. It has been called one of the most remarkable and beautiful churches of the 19th century.

ABOVE: *The design for the chancel of St Mary's. Burges often commissioned watercolour perspectives of his proposed schemes from the artist Axel Haig. These could be exhibited, and also gave clients an idea of the completed scheme.*

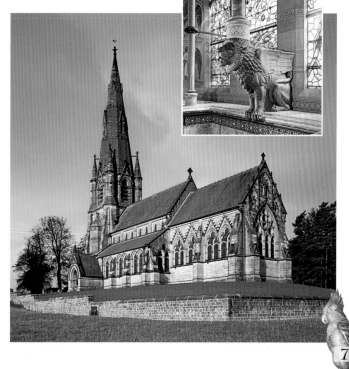

CARDIFF CASTLE

For the 38-year-old Burges, the rebuilding of Cardiff Castle must have been a dream commission. His client, the young 3rd Marquess of Bute, who became a personal friend, was as great an enthusiast of the Middle Ages as Burges himself. Moreover, Bute was one of the richest men of his day, and quite prepared to spend lavishly on his Welsh castle. Bute was the most important figure in South Wales, where his industrial interests were paying for his architectural pleasures. The rebuilding of the castle caused a sensation when Burges's plans were first made known. Not everybody was delighted – Burges's ideas caused consternation at first, with one antiquary grumbling to another, 'We shall soon have the old place ruined …'.

Plans for the castle were first drawn up in 1865, and continued for the rest of Burges's life. The castle was gradually transformed from an historic but somewhat dreary mansion into a Gothic feudal extravaganza. Lord Bute's enthusiasm for fantasy interiors equalled Burges's, and the castle contains many rooms that must have been impractical to use, but great fun to create.

ABOVE: *Burges's eye-catching Clock Tower at Cardiff Castle is eclectic in style, and its colourful statues and heraldry draw inspiration from the medieval period.*

The first part of the scheme was the Clock Tower. It was designed only for occasional use, but its interiors are packed with decoration. Both Burges's and Lord Bute's ideas and interests appear in iconography drawn from biblical, classical and historical sources. Like Burges, Lord and Lady Bute were fond of travel to foreign countries, where they gleaned ideas for the castle.

LEFT: *Burges built upwards in a series of extraordinary towers of differing shape and size, giving the castle an interestingly varied skyline.*

ABOVE: *Burges loved to include grotesques or mythical beasts in his schemes.*

LEFT: *Burges designed every aspect of an interior. The Summer Smoking Room is suffused with decoration in tiles, mural painting, stained glass, metalwork and textiles.*

STATE VIRESCO

earlier part of the castle interior Burges sometimes demolished a number of smaller rooms to create a more impressive space, such as the Banqueting Hall. Here, in the 15th-century part of the building, Burges's designs are adapted to that period. He was prepared to be sensitive to earlier periods when he desired, and would make an effort to incorporate original material into a 'restoration'.

Burges's interiors were not always a complete success. The Grand Staircase that he began at the castle in 1874 was felt to be too large and the stairs too steep. Work stopped, and it remained unfinished until it was demolished in 1927.

Burges's death in 1881 was a great loss to the Butes, who referred to him as 'the soul-inspiring one'. Cardiff Castle was not finally completed for another ten years, and interiors such as the Arab and Chaucer Rooms had to be finished by Burges's brother-in-law, R.P. Pullan.

The Arab Room was inspired by Arab architecture in Sicily, and its glorious ceiling is covered in pure gold leaf. This use of expensive materials is typical of Burges and Bute, who were inclined to disregard cost in favour of effect. Most of the rooms at Cardiff were designed to impress, and when converting the

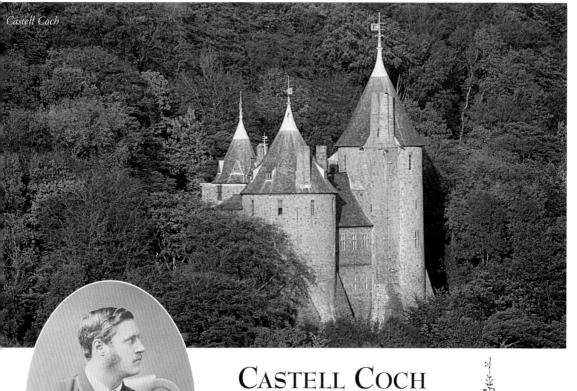

CASTELL COCH

C astell Coch (Welsh for 'the red castle') stands on a thickly wooded hillside to the north of Cardiff, and is surely Burges's most picturesque building. Its circular towers, topped by conical roofs, seem to bring a Wagnerian flavour to the Taff Valley.

It was originally a medieval fortress, but by the 19th century had fallen into complete ruin. The castle stands on the Marquess of Bute's estate, and in 1871 Lord Bute asked Burges to report on its state and make recommendations as to what might be done with it. Burges conducted a thorough archaeological dig, and reported to Bute the following year. He suggested that there were two courses open – either to leave the castle as it was, making only a few repairs, or to take a more drastic course, that of a complete restoration. Burges had the idea that Bute and his family might use Castell Coch as an occasional summer residence. Lord Bute approved the idea of an archaeological restoration and work began in 1875. The Well Tower, Kitchen Tower and Keep Tower, as well as a huge curtain wall,

ABOVE:
The 3rd Marquess of Bute (1847–1900) was Burges's greatest patron. He shared his architect's passion for the medieval world, and by his early 20s had commissioned the restoration of two castles in Wales.

RIGHT: *Burges was a great admirer of Viollet-le-Duc's work on medieval architecture and design, and copied many of his ideas at Castell Coch as well as elsewhere.*

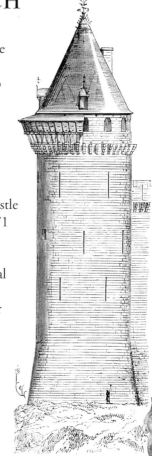

11

ABOVE: *The murals in the Upper Hall of Castell Coch, showing the life and martyrdoms of British saints, was painted by Lonsdale. It was the only interior completed before Burges's death.*

RIGHT: *Lady Bute's extraordinary bedroom was completed after Burges's death in 1881 from 'spinal myelitis'. The furniture was added by his assistant John Chapple a decade later.*

were all rebuilt, and Burges incorporated original fabric into his recreation. A fully working drawbridge and portcullis were built. He sought precedents from other Welsh castles but, as always, was inspired by French Gothic. Burges was much influenced by the restorer of French medieval architecture, Viollet-le-Duc. Another source of inspiration was the 13th-century Swiss castle of Chillon, on Lake Geneva.

Burges – with considerable understatement – wrote that inside Castell Coch he had 'ventured to indulge in a little more ornament'. The Drawing Room, with its magnificent domed ceiling, is a wonderful interior, although its decoration was not finished until some years after Burges's death. Lord Bute's bedroom is small and spartan, but Lady Bute's circular bedroom is magnificent, set beneath a glorious mirrored dome. The family very rarely used Castell Coch, making only occasional trips during their short season in South Wales.

KNIGHTSHAYES COURT

ABOVE: *Knightshayes, viewed from the south. A number of Gothic Revival country houses were built in the 1860s and 1870s; Knightshayes is a unique example by Burges.*

Burges only ever built three major houses. Two of these were town houses (one of which was for himself), but the magnificent Knightshayes Court, built on the hills overlooking nearby Tiverton, in Devon, was his only country house commission.

Knightshayes was begun for Burges's patron John Heathcoat Amory in 1869. The choice of Burges as architect was an odd one, as Heathcoat Amory was not an ardent medievalist like Lord Bute, but a hunting squire whose wealth was drawn from a large lace manufactory in Tiverton. It seems appropriate, therefore, that Burges's design for Knightshayes was originally described as 'stately and bold, and its medievalism is not obtrusive'.

Knightshayes is a large, three-storied house, built of red Hensley stone. The south front commands a magnificent view over the parkland. The more modest and asymmetric entrance front on the north side was originally intended to have a large tower, but once the design was modified, work progressed rapidly.

By the end of 1873, the house was habitable but undecorated. Burges now wanted to go ahead with his elaborate and detailed plans for the interiors. These were, of course, quite splendid – an extravagant design in stained glass, carved wood, stonework and painted decoration, all in Burges's customary medieval style. The prospect of the huge expense involved in this scheme must have thoroughly unnerved the family and, within a short time, Burges seems to have been dismissed from the project. Although some work to the interiors had begun, the decorative finishes had not, so the house had a Burges structure, with certain ceilings and stone carvings designed by him, but little else. In the Great Hall, for example, the stained glass was never installed and his delightful stone corbels remain unpainted.

The fashionable – but rather less extravagant – decorator J.D. Crace was employed to complete the interiors, which he did during the late 1870s and early 1880s. Crace's scheme was also in the Gothic style, but less robust and extreme than Burges's. Consequently, it was considerably cheaper.

Knightshayes Court illustrates attitudes to Burges's work during the 20th century. The Heathcoat Amory

family modified the Victorian Gothic look of the house in the Edwardian period, and this accelerated during the 1950s, when appreciation of Victorian Gothic was at an all-time low. In 1972 the family gave Knightshayes to The National Trust, coinciding with a revival of interest in the period. Ceilings were uncovered, and original features reinstated. In recent years, the library has been restored and one of Burges's unexecuted bedroom schemes has been recreated in order to give an impression of how the house might have looked, had Burges not been the victim of his own opulent style.

ABOVE: *The Great Hall. Here, Burges evoked a noble hall of the Middle Ages for the Heathcoat Amory family.*

LEFT: *A sculptured detail from Knightshayes. Burges was dismissed from the project before his sculpture could be painted.*

TOWER HOUSE

RIGHT: *Melbury Road, Kensington, was something of an 'artists' colony', with many imaginative houses in this area. None is more striking than Tower House, which Burges designed for himself.*

BELOW RIGHT: *This detail is from the mermaid chimney-piece in Burges's own bedroom.*

ABOVE: *The 'Golden' bed was designed for the guest bedroom in Tower House. It is covered in gold leaf and decorated with paintings, mirrors and enamelled glass.*

For many years, Burges lived in rooms attached to his office in London's Buckingham Street. These small and overcrowded quarters were a repository for his collection of books, armour and objets d'art. His rooms were crammed not only with objects, but with dogs as well. Burges adored animals, but his friends and clients had to put up with uneven canine tempers! He decorated the rooms with murals and designed furniture and metalwork for his own use. Tables were laden with glittering *bibelots*, many of which he actually used. One visitor described a tea party with William Burges: '… the meal served in beaten gold, the cream poured out of a single onyx, and the tea strictured in its descent on account of real rubies in the pot.'

After some years, Burges decided to build himself a house in Melbury Road, Kensington. He began work on Tower House in 1876, and moved in two years later. The house is built of red brick, and has a tower with a conical roof – it is as if Castell Coch has reappeared in a London suburb. Although Tower House isn't large, it was described as 'a palace of art', packed with treasures. Burges's interiors are usually dominated by an impressive chimneypiece or ceiling, and there is no lack of either at Tower House. The painted stone chimney-pieces are Burges's finest, and each room is lit by stained glass. The dining room ceiling is painted with his beloved signs of the zodiac. The library and drawing room inter-connect, and are decorated with themes such as learning and literature.

Upstairs, the 'Golden' or guest's room has painted butterflies fluttering in circles upon the ceiling, while frogs and mice do battle on the beams.

Burges designed all the gilded furniture for the room. Next door is the 'Mermaid' bedroom, which was his own room, and here the walls and chimneypiece have an underwater theme, perhaps inspired by Burges's own collection of Japanese woodcuts.

It was in this room that Burges died in April 1881. He had enjoyed Tower House for only three years. It stayed in the possession of the Burges family until its contents were sold in 1933. The house still remains a private residence.

BURGES'S FURNITURE

BELOW: *The Great Bookcase now at Knightshayes Court was designed by Burges for himself c.1859–62. Many of his artist friends collaborated on the panels, which illustrate biblical and classical scenes.*

Furniture of the mid-Victorian period tended to be solid and showy, with expensive veneers of richly figured wood and sometimes abundantly carved in a variety of different styles. Anything less appropriate for an interior designed by William Burges cannot be imagined. His bright, colourful decorative schemes needed complementary furnishings. Burges himself wrote that the great feature of a medieval chamber would have been the furniture, which he said 'would be covered with paintings, both ornaments and subjects; it not only did its duty as furniture, but spoke and told a story'.

Burges intended making such painted furniture, to complete his stunning interiors. His designs date from the late 1850s, but he first exhibited it to the public at the International Exhibition in London in 1862, displaying examples in the 'Medieval Court'.

To conventional Victorians, used to a high finish and glossy veneers, Burges's 'medieval' furniture must have seemed incomprehensible – crude and garish. The furniture was usually made from fairly rough

ABOVE: *Burges's dressing table (1867). Burges often favoured red for his furniture; he would also incorporate marble or mosaic into the design or – as in this example – tiny mirrors and paintings of girls he admired!*

LEFT: *The Library at Cardiff Castle contains all of its original furniture, and is the only complete interior by Burges in existence.*

softwood, but was then carefully and delightfully painted and gilded. Appropriately, the result has been called 'Pre-Raphaelite furniture'. As always, Burges found a limited number of clients, and his finest decorated pieces were made for himself. Not all of his furniture was painted and items made for Cardiff Castle, Worcester College and a few other clients were decorated with carving and marquetry.

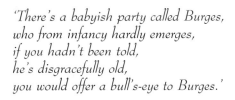

Burges's own particular brand of humour often appears in his furniture, and pieces such as his own wardrobe and chests were painted with bizarre anthropomorphic scissors or shaving brushes with heads! A lively sense of the comic was said to be his most marked characteristic, and his friend Rossetti wrote of him:

*'There's a babyish party called Burges,
who from infancy hardly emerges,
if you hadn't been told,
he's disgracefully old,
you would offer a bull's-eye to Burges.'*

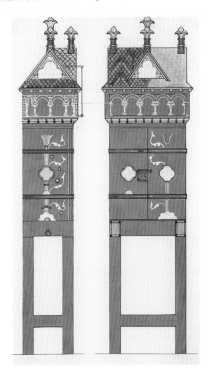

ABOVE: *Burges's pieces sometimes look somewhat architectural, but they were inspired by surviving examples of medieval French furniture.*

Burges's furniture is now rare and highly sought-after by both museums and private collectors.

Textiles and Metalwork

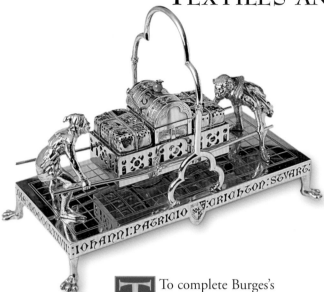

ABOVE: *Lord Bute's cruet was made in 1877. Two figures in medieval costume carry the condiments in this highly imaginative piece.*

RIGHT: *Burges gave this gold and enamel brooch to Lady Bute in 1873. She was so delighted that she wrote a description to her sister, saying that Burges was 'a duck'!*

T To complete Burges's evocation of a perfect 13th-century room, two further elements were needed – textiles and metalwork.

Burges had researched antique textiles in museums all over Europe, and concluded that those of the medieval period were both colourful and elaborate. He also knew that textiles were an important part of life in a noble house of the Middle Ages; therefore, he occasionally designed hangings, covers and costume for his interior schemes, although few survive today. His textiles were made of wool, velvet or silk, and were hand-embroidered and embellished with spangles, precious metals and, in some cases, gemstones. The effect was precisely what Burges wanted – rich and splendid. This love of rich effects is perhaps best and most enduringly found in his metalwork, which is certainly the most imaginative of

the Victorian Gothic Revival. Architectural fittings, church furnishings and chandeliers are among his more practical items.

However, it is for his precious metalwork that Burges is justly celebrated. Burges loved the romance of precious stones and jewels. He deplored the mass-produced and – to his mind – tasteless items commercially available in the 1860s. Taking medieval originals as his model, but adding touches of his own humorous imagination, Burges designed goblets, flasks, decanters, crosses, cutlery and jewellery. As usual, he was his own best client, and many items bear the name 'William Burges' in enamel. He made a serious attempt to revive medieval techniques, and he occasionally incorporated antique gems or curios into his own designs. He favoured the London firm of Barkentin and Kraal to undertake his commissions, and they produced some superbly crafted items from his designs. His church plate gave him the opportunity to produce something that looked authentically medieval, but even these have the distinctive touch of Burges's imagination. His use of handcrafted techniques, and of cabochon or uncut stones, is perhaps Burges's greatest legacy to later designers. From the 1890s, the artists of the Arts and Crafts movement relied on the methods Burges had so keenly encouraged.